DATE DUE

*V*isiting the *P*ast

Pompeii and Herculaneum

John and Elizabeth Seely

Heinemann Library
Chicago, Illinois

© 2000 Reed Educational & Professional Publishing
Published by Heinemann Library,
an imprint of Reed Educational & Professional Publishing,
100 N. LaSalle, Suite 1010
Chicago, IL 60602

Customer Service 888-454-2279

Designed by Visual Image
Illustrations by Visual Image
Printed in Hong Kong

04 03 02 01 00
10 9 8 7 6 5 4 3 2 1

Library of Congress Cataloging-in-Publication Data
Seely, John, 1941-
    Pompeii & Herculaneum / John and Elizabeth Seely.
        p. cm. – (Visiting the past)
    Includes bibliographical references and index.
    Summary: Describes the design, economy, food and drink, homes,
gardens, cultures, destruction, and ruins of Pompeii and Herculaneum,
the two cities buried by the eruption of Mount Vesuvius.
    ISBN 1-57572-859-1 (lib. bdg.)
    1. Pompeii (Extinct city)—Juvenile literature. 2. Herculaneum
(Extinct city) Juvenile literature. [1. Pompeii (Extinct city)
2. Herculaneum (Extinct city) 3. Vesuvius (Italy)—Eruption, 79.
4. Italy—Antiquities.] I. Seely, Elizabeth, 1936- . II. Title.
III. Title: Pompeii and Herculaneum. IV. Series.
DG70.P7S47 1999
937'.7—dc21   99-25555
                                                   CIP

Acknowledgments
The Publishers would like to thank John Seely for permission to reproduce all photographs.

Cover photograph reproduced with permission of Robert Harding Picture Library.

Every effort has been made to contact copyright holders of any material reproduced in this book.
Any omissions will be rectified in subsequent printings if notice is given to the publisher.

Some words are shown in bold, **like this.** You can find out what they
mean by looking in the glossary.

Contents

Two Cities of Vesuvius

The coast of Italy south of Naples is a popular vacation destination. Every summer tourists flock to resorts like Sorrento, Positano, and Amalfi, and the beaches are packed. Around 3,000 years ago, this area—known as Campania—was already attracting visitors, and, in the 8th century B.C., merchants from Greece set up trading posts in two small villages called Pompeii and Herculaneum.

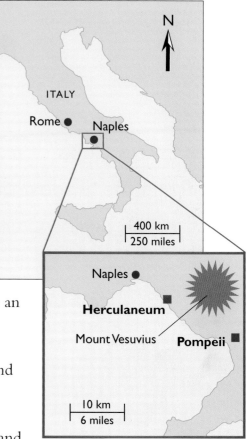

Pompeii was on a river close to the sea. Boats carried goods between its harbor and ports around the Mediterranean. It soon became an important center for trade. Herculaneum was a smaller settlement used by traders from nearby Neapolis, or Naples. Both towns were wealthy and attracted the attention of invaders. They were occupied first by the Etruscans, and then by the Samnites, fierce warriors from the mountains inland.

But an even more powerful enemy was looking greedily at this rich and fertile area. About 136 miles (220 kilometers) north of Pompeii was the city and **republic** of Rome. In the middle of the 4th century B.C. the Romans invaded Campania. Between 310 and 302 B.C., they captured both Pompeii and Herculaneum.

This is the Italian coast south of Naples

4

Growing prosperity

For nearly four centuries, the two towns grew and became prosperous. Wealthy citizens from Naples liked to have seaside homes in Herculaneum, while Pompeii remained an important trading post. It became a center for many different industries, including the making of woollen cloth.

This is the Bay of Naples and Mt Vesuvius.

Judging by its size, and the houses that have been excavated, by A.D. 62, Pompeii probably had a population of about 20,000—a large town by the standards of the time. It was home to businessmen, lawyers and doctors, working families, shopkeepers, and slaves. But in that year something happened that threatened to change the lives of the inhabitants of both towns forever. This is how it was described by Seneca, a writer of the time:

"Pompeii, the famous city in Campania, has been laid low by an earthquake. A flock of hundreds of sheep was killed, statues were cracked, and some people were so shocked that they wandered about as if deprived of their wits."

Here is a married couple from Pompeii. They are believed to be the lawyer Terentius Neo and his wife.

In the Shadow of the Volcano

Every morning when they got up, the citizens of Pompeii and Herculaneum faced the reason for the destruction of A.D. 62. Immediately to the north towers Mount Vesuvius, an active volcano. It is one of a chain of volcanoes that stretches down the Italian coast as far as Sicily and the famous peaks of Stromboli and Etna.

Vesuvius rumbled and heaved in the year 62, but it did not erupt. People set about rebuilding their shattered towns. They made rapid progress, and life soon returned to normal. But worse was to follow. Seventeen years later, early on the morning of August 24, A.D. 79, the people of Pompeii felt the earth shake violently beneath them. Terrified, they looked toward Vesuvius and saw the mountain explode. Flames leaped into the sky followed by an umbrella cloud of poisonous smoke. Pieces of red-hot rock and dense clouds of ash began to cascade down onto the town.

The ash was thick, and it formed a blanket that quickly rose up the sides of the houses. People began to panic. Some of them tried to hide inside their houses, while others ran out of the town toward the sea. But the ash and the poisonous fumes were deadly. From the human remains that have been found, it is estimated that at least 2,000 people, one-tenth of the population, were killed.

While the rest of the people tried to escape, the ash and rocks continued to fall until the whole of Pompeii was buried under a layer fourteen or fifteen feet (four or five meters) deep. The ash covered everything, houses, gardens, streets, animals, and people.

Here, Vesuvius looms above the town of Pompeii.

Herculaneum's fate

Herculaneum escaped the ash and the rocks, only to suffer a different fate. The eruption threw up huge jets of steam, which reached temperatures approaching 1,800°F (1,000°C). As the steam cooled, it turned into rain that mixed with the ash and rocks already on the ground to make a river of boiling mud. The mud flowed down the mountainside and covered the city. Most of the people had already fled, but the few who stayed were killed by the mudslide. When the mud cooled, it turned into solid rock up to 60 feet (18 meters) deep!

This painting from Pompeii shows Bacchus, the god of wine, and Vesuvius planted with vines.

This man and child tried to escape but were overcome and died near one of the gates of Pompeii. **Archaeologists** made plaster casts of the impressions left by their bodies in the hardened mud.

7

The Buried Cities

Immediately after the eruption, the Roman authorities helped the survivors find new homes. There were some attempts to rescue valuables from Pompeii—as is shown by **graffiti** scratched on the ruins. But there was nothing that could be done to rescue the two cities. They remained hidden in the mud for over 1,500 years.

The remains of Pompeii were discovered by accident in 1594, but they were not systematically **excavated** until the eighteenth century. Even then, people were more interested in finding and taking away statues, **mosaics,** and other beautiful objects than in trying to understand the lives of the people who had lived in the city. Gradually, however, **archaeologists** uncovered the city and began to realize what a wonderful historical record lay beneath their feet.

Herculaneum was much more difficult to excavate than Pompeii because of the great depth of solid rock that covered it. Also, a modern town now stands over much of the site. Even today, only a small part of Herculaneum has been excavated.

Frozen in time

Pompeii provides us with a fascinating picture of town life during the first century A.D. It is possible now to visit the site and stroll around the streets, just as if you were in a modern town. You can go into houses and shops that look much the same as they must have nearly 2,000 years ago. Some of the houses still have the beautiful paintings and mosaics that decorated them when Vesuvius erupted. In the wine shops, you can see the jars that were filled with wine. In the bakery, the grain mills and bread ovens remain undamaged. In one bakery, archaeologists even found charred loaves that were being baked.

The site of Pompeii is about 3,900 feet (1,200 meters) long by 2,300 feet (700 meters) wide. It was a planned town with streets forming a grid. The two main streets were the Via dell'Abbondanza, which ran from east to west, and the Via Stabiana, which ran from north to south. Names given streets and buildings are modern ones, usually in Italian; we don't know the original names. In the southwest corner of the town were the great **forum** and the main public buildings. The rest of the town spread out to the east and the north.

Many of the houses on this street in Herculaneum are in good shape because they were protected by the volcanic rock.

Vesuvius is visible from this street in Pompeii.

9

The Town Center

Most people who visit Pompeii today arrive first at the **forum**. This was the great open square where people would meet to talk and carry on their business. The forum was very big, over 492 feet (150 meters) long and nearly 130 feet (40 meters) wide. It was the equivalent of a modern downtown, though it was actually at one end of the town.

This is the forum at Pompeii. The building on the right is the Temple of Jupiter, the most important religious building in the town. The white columns at the far end are the remains of the **colonnade** and gallery that surrounded the forum on three sides. These columns supported a roofed and shaded walkway where people could shelter from the sun in summer and the rain in winter. In midsummer, temperatures regularly rise above 86°F or 30°C.

Around the forum

At the far end of the forum are the remains of the offices of the **duovirii** and the **aediles.** The *duovirii,* or magistrates, were the two most important officials and were elected each year to administer justice. The *aediles* were responsible for the streets and sanitation, the markets, and the games. There was also an office for the members of the town council.

Around the sides of the forum were other temples and important public buildings. One of these was the **basilica.** We know this because someone scratched the word "basilica" on one of the walls before it was destroyed by the earthquake of A.D. 62. The basilica was a great hall, similar to the main halls of the private houses of wealthy men. It was used as a meeting place for businessmen and lawyers. Law cases were discussed and decided and business deals were arranged. At other times, the basilica was used for meetings and other social events.

The basilica was a large building with tall columns, like this one (below). Many **archaeologists** believe the columns supported a heavy timber roof to protect people from the weather.

Near the Temple of Jupiter was the **macellum** (above). Although Pompeii had many shops selling all kinds of produce, the macellum was the main food market where fruit, vegetables, and meat could be bought. It also housed a large fish market and a place for changing money.

Earning a Living

Pompeii was the center of a prosperous farming area famed for its cattle, which produced abundant milk, and sheep, which provided wool to be made into cloth. The town had many shops selling local food, drinks, and manufactured goods. However, because Pompeii had started as a center for international trade and remained one under the Romans, goods from many different countries also found their way into its shops. Pottery was imported from France, and when **archaeologists** cleared the town, they found a crate of French pottery waiting to be unpacked.

The main commercial area ran along the Via dell'Abbondanza. Here were not only bars and restaurants, but also shops and workshops. Often a building would contain a workshop, a shop, and living quarters for the owner and his family. The manufacture of woolen cloth was important.

Verecundus's felt-making shop was in the Via dell'Abbondanza.

At the **fullonica** of Stephanus, the new cloth was placed in large vats like this one and treated with soda, **potash**, **fuller's earth,** and human urine. Stephanus even placed a large jar outside his shop and invited passing men to help fill it!

Working with cloth

Wool from sheep was brought into town and processed by artisans such as Stephanus and Verecundus, who have been identified by their shops. After the wool was spun and woven into cloth, it had to be cleaned and dyed. Stephanus owned a large workshop, called a fullonica, where new cloth was washed. After cleaning, the cloth was dyed, using vegetable dyes. The fullonica was also used as a laundry for dirty clothes.

Across the road was the workshop and shop where Verecundus made and sold felt for blankets, hats, and slippers. He was clearly a successful businessman and had large pictures painted on the outside of his shop to advertise his wares.

Other trades in the town included perfume-making, carpentry, plumbing, and wheel-making. There were also several bakeries.

At the bakery of Modestus, large stone mills were used to grind corn. The lower half of such a mill was a large cone-shaped stone. A hollow stone, shaped to fit, rested over the cone, and the grain was poured in at the top. As the top stone was turned by slaves or donkeys, the grain was ground between the two stones. It came out at the bottom as wholemeal flour. After the flour had been made into dough, the circular, flat loaves of bread were baked in a brick oven.

Eating and Drinking

Food and drink were very important to the people of Pompeii. Despite the violence of the eruption that buried the town, the remains of many different foods were found in shops and homes. Food shops sold fruit and vegetables, dried goods such as beans and chickpeas, plus meat, fish, cereals, milk, and wine.

The vineyards on the slopes of Vesuvius produced a good white wine, called Vesuvium. The area is still famous today for its wine. Wine was made at farms and villas near Pompeii, and was sold by the town's wine merchants. A person wanting to have a drink would go to a bar like the **thermopolium** of Asellina. Food was also on sale, and some bars offered live entertainment, provided by dancers. Customers also could pass the time in gambling games.

This shop in Herculaneum sold cereals and wine.

Fruit grows well around Pompeii. This painting shows pomegranates, which still grow in the gardens there.

Local speciality

Pompeii was also famous for the making of a special fish sauce, called **garum**. This sauce was highly prized by the Romans and widely used in cooking, as we know from many writers of the time. Garum was made from sardines and other small fish. The fish were gutted and the guts were mixed in a vat with chopped fish and eggs and then pounded to produce a pulp. The vats were left in the sun for several weeks, so that the mixture fermented and some of the liquid evaporated. Then the pulp was strained and the liquid used as a sauce. Not surprisingly, the factories where garum was made produced a smell that not everyone found pleasant—the writer Seneca complained bitterly about it!

The thermopolium of Asellina had a long marble counter with circular holes in it. These were to hold the **amphorae,** which were long jars with bases that were pointed rather than flat. In summer the wine was served cool, but in winter people preferred it hot.

Fish was a popular food, and wealthy people spent a lot of money on large and expensive fish. This **mosaic** shows some of the fish that could be caught in the sea near Pompeii.

The City Streets

As you wander around Pompeii, it is strange to think that you are walking along the same pavements and streets as people did over 2,000 years ago. The roads are paved with slabs of gray, volcanic rock from Vesuvius—just as the streets of nearby Naples are today. The pavements were a lot higher than the level of the road, for a very good reason. Not only did the road act as a drain for rainwater, but it also carried away a lot of rubbish and even sewage. This made it rather unpleasant to cross, so stepping-stones were built into the road to help people keep their feet clean. Herculaneum, however, had a sewage system that ran under the streets, so there was no need for stepping-stones.

Pompeii's stepping-stones were arranged with gaps so that the wheels of carts could pass between them. We know that the streets of Pompeii carried a lot of wheeled traffic, because there are deep grooves worn into the stone. Herculaneum, on the other hand, seems to have had little wheeled traffic. This difference was probably because Herculaneum was much less of a manufacturing and trading center than Pompeii.

This street in Pompeii had stepping-stones so that people could cross the road without getting their feet wet.

A manhole cover in Herculaneum led to the sewer under the road.

16

A good water supply is very important to any city, and Pompeii had excellent water. It was piped from springs in the hills and fed into large, raised tanks. It was carried from these through lead pipes to the larger houses and also to fountains, which were placed at regular intervals along the streets. Many fountains were carved with the heads of humans or animals.

These wheel ruts show that many carts must have used this road in Pompeii.

The head of the god Neptune has been carved on this fountain in Herculaneum.

17

Beautiful Homes

Many of the ordinary working people of Pompeii lived in small houses like those on the Via dell'Abbondanza, but both Pompeii and Herculaneum also had many large and beautiful houses. They have given **archaeologists** and historians a very detailed picture of how people lived and how the shape and design of houses changed during the towns' history.

The houses were very different from those of today. The larger houses had few windows looking out into the street. Instead, they were built around one or more courtyards or gardens, and daylight came into the house from these. A typical house was entered from the street into an open space called the **atrium**.

Many houses had impressive doorways, like this one at Herculaneum.

The atrium was usually partly roofed, but the section open to the sky let in light and rain. Beneath the opening, a stone tank, called the **impluvium**, collected the water for use.

Around the atrium were small rooms, including bedrooms, and often a larger room, which was used as a dining room, called the **triclinium**. Kitchen arrangements were often very primitive. The kitchen was a small room, containing a sink and a brick oven. It was often only big enough for one slave to work in. There was no chimney, and the smoke just went out through a hole in the roof. This was not only unpleasant, because the kitchen filled with smoke, but it was also dangerous. Many house fires were caused in this way.

Here are cooking tools from a house in Pompeii.

The windows of the rooms did not usually have glass, so, at night and when the weather was bad, they were closed with shutters. Closed rooms were dark and stuffy. The only light was provided by naked flames—tapers, candles, or lamps. It takes 100 candles to give the same light as one modern light bulb, so it is not surprising that records told that people who spent a lot of time reading often suffered serious eye problems.

The family often placed the shrine to their household gods, called the **lararium**, in or near the atrium. This is the lararium of a wealthy Pompeii family named Vettii.

Beautiful Gardens

The Romans loved gardens, and many of the larger houses at Pompeii and Herculaneum had large, enclosed gardens. From the **atrium,** another doorway led into a larger open space surrounded by an open veranda supported by columns. Such an enclosed garden was known as the **peristyle**.

Archaeologists have discovered a lot about the trees, shrubs, and plants that these gardens contained. There were such fruit trees as pears, figs, and pomegranates, as well as vines trained over **pergolas**. Roses flourished, and in the spring there were violets and hyacinths. Some houses also had a vegetable garden. We know from writers of the time that people grew lettuce, peas, and brussels sprouts.

Loreius Tiburtinus, who owned this house (right), was a priest of the Temple of Isis. The followers of this goddess believed that water symbolized life, so he had a stream running through his garden with a carved fountain in the center.

The peristyle formed an enclosed garden (left) surrounded by rooms, which opened onto it. This is the garden of the House of the Painted Venus. It is called that because of the paintings on the wall at the back.

Running water

As you might expect in a country that was very hot in summer, people liked to have water features in their gardens. They had little streams, fountains, and artificial waterfalls. Other decorations included marble statues and **sundials**.

The House of Neptune and Amphitrite at Herculaneum had a beautifully decorated inner courtyard used for meals in the summer.

Many house owners liked to continue their gardens into their houses by having garden paintings on the walls. These paintings give us a vivid idea of what their gardens were like. This painting is from the House of the Painted Venus.

Having a Good Time

The citizens of Pompeii liked to enjoy themselves. They were enthusiastic theatergoers, so it is not surprising that there were two theaters in the town. The large theater was probably built in about 200 B.C. Like many theaters in Greece, where dramatic productions first developed, it was built on a slope and looked out toward open countryside, which provided a natural background for the plays.

Smaller performances of plays, mimes, music, and recitations took place in the Odeon, the small theater. Built more than a hundred years after the large theater, it could hold about 1,000 people.

The large theater at Pompeii seated up to 5,000 people, who came to see Greek and Roman tragedies and comedies. Plays were held in daylight.

This **mosaic** of musicians shows a scene from a comedy.

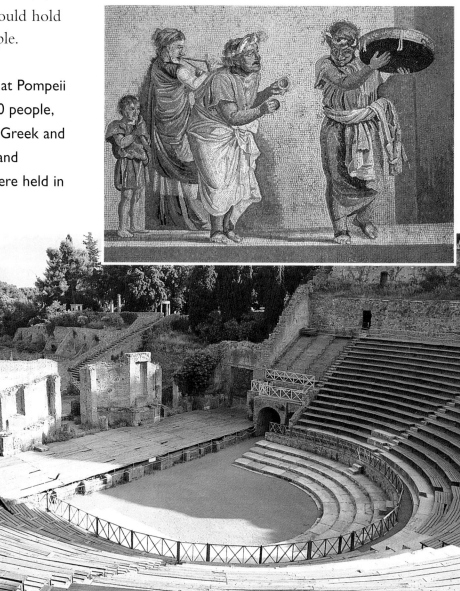

Dangerous games

Romans liked the theater, but they loved watching fighting even more. At about the same time as the Odeon was built, work started on a huge **amphitheater** where the people of Pompeii went to watch **gladiators**. These were slaves or prisoners of war who had been trained as professional fighters. Many different types of combat were staged in the amphitheater. They held fights on horseback, fights with swords and **tridents**, and encounters between gladiators and wild animals, including bulls, wild boar, or even bears. **Graffiti** in the amphitheater announces, "Felix will fight bears." Fights were to the death. When one gladiator had another at his mercy, he would turn to the magistrates in charge of the games to ask whether he should kill him or not. Sometimes the decision was left to the crowd. The animals were shown no mercy.

The amphitheater at Pompeii was perhaps large enough to seat the entire population. The whole building was 460 feet by 345 feet (140 by 105 meters) and the arena is nearly 230 feet (70 meters) long. Because the theater had no roof, an awning was put up to shade the audience. Graffiti advertising the games announced "There will be awnings."

The games at the amphitheater were as popular as football games are today—and sometimes there was trouble in the stands. This painting from Pompeii shows a riot between the people of Pompeii and visiting fans from the nearby city of Nuceria in A.D. 59. Several Nucerians were killed, and the games were banned for ten years.

23

The Body Beautiful

Another cruel sport the people of Pompeii enjoyed was **cockfighting**. This took place not at the **amphitheater** but at the **palaestrum** nearby. The palaestrum was not built mainly for blood sports. It was really a huge, open-air sports center, where the young men of the town went to train for sports and to keep fit. The young men were encouraged to be well-behaved and disciplined by the Augustan Youth Movement, which organized games and athletic competitions as well as horseback parades through the town.

Cockfighting attracted gamblers. This **mosaic** of a cockfight shows the bag of money that has been bet on the fight.

Visiting the baths

Hygiene, too, was very important. Some of the larger houses had their own bathrooms, but many did not. The city provided a number of public bathhouses, which were open from noon until late in the evening. Any citizen could use them, and they were very popular. Some had separate sections for men and women. At others, men and women had to bathe at different times.

At the palaestrum at Pompeii, young men prepared for a variety of athletic events and other games, and used the large swimming pool visible on the right. Like a modern pool, it had a shallow end and a deep end.

A visit to a bathhouse took a person through several rooms and pools. First came the dressing room, called the **apodyterium**. This was followed by a series of rooms, each one warmer than the last. The first was the **frigidarium**, or cold room. The lukewarm **tepidarium** came next, and then on to the **caldarium**, the hot room. Here there was a hot bath, in which bathers could immerse themselves, after which they dunked themselves in a cold basin to cool down again. The bathers didn't use soap; instead they had oil, **soda,** and body scrapers.

People didn't go to the baths just to get clean. They went to meet friends, have a chat, and catch up on the latest gossip while they had some food and drink. Most bathers took at least one slave to help them, so the rooms must have been very crowded.

The apodyterium of the women's baths at Herculaneum (above) is decorated with a large mosaic and has shelves for the bathers' clothes.

Here is the caldarium of the women's baths at Herculaneum

Personal Beliefs

The Romans believed in many different gods, most of whom they had taken over from Greek religion. Probably the god most frequently mentioned and depicted in Pompeii was Venus, the goddess of love and the mother of all nature. Her name often appears in **graffiti** scrawled on walls by young men who felt that they had been badly treated by their girlfriends. Verecundus the felt-maker had a picture of Venus on the wall outside his shop, and one wealthy family had a large painting of Venus arising from the sea on their garden wall.

All these gods were worshiped in their temples. They were part of the official religion of the Roman Empire. But many people in Pompeii wanted a more personal religion that would give their lives meaning and hope, so they turned to what are called mystery religions.

One of the Greek gods the Romans adopted was Apollo, the god of peace and truth, whose temple and statue were on one side of the **forum**.

Animals were sacrificed to the gods on special occasions. In this carving, the priests prepare for a sacrifice.

The worship of Isis

One of the most popular mystery religions was the worship of Isis, the Egyptian goddess of fertility. She was the wife and sister of Osiris, the god of the Underworld, where people went when they died, and the judge of the dead. The followers of Isis believed that if they lived their lives in the right way and attended services at her temple, they would be rewarded by life after death. Paintings and other evidence from the Temple of Isis at Pompeii have told us a lot about this religion.

Such beliefs were very important, especially because people's lives were so short. Medical science was primitive, and many people did not live much beyond 40 years of age. People prepared for death by planning and paying for large and elaborate tombs. As one comic writer of the time said, "It makes no sense to decorate the house you live in now, but not the one where you'll spend so much longer."

Tombs were built outside the city walls (right). These are near the Nucerian Gate at Pompeii.

The Temple of Isis was open every day. The highlight of the day's worship was the afternoon service of the blessing and offering of water, the source of all life, shown in this painting (left).

27

Timeline

8th century B.C.	Greeks establish a trading post at Pompeii and a settlement at Herculaneum, probably on the sites of earlier villages.
c.520 B.C.–c.425 B.C.	Campania, the area around Pompeii and Herculaneum, is invaded first by the Etruscans and then by the Samnites.
c.425 B.C.–c.350 B.C.	Period of peace and prosperity, under Samnite rule
c.343 B.C.	Romans begin their invasion of Campania.
310 B.C.–302 B.C.	Pompeii and Herculaneum are occupied by the Romans. Both towns are made allied cities, which means that they can use their own language, control their own trade, and elect their own magistrates.
2nd century B.C.	The **forum** is laid out as we see it today. The temple of Jupiter, **basilica,** and large theater are built.
91 B.C.	Pompeii and Herculaneum join the rebellion against Rome. Both cities are besieged by Sulla and conquered.
80 B.C.	Pompeii is placed under the direct rule of Rome. Many Romans move to the city and settle there. Sulla's nephew, Publius Sulla, becomes the city's leading citizen and patron. Many new buildings are put up, and the city grows in size and wealth. Buildings in Pompeii that date from this period include the forum baths, the **amphitheater,** and the Odeon. Herculaneum does not grow at the same rate because Romans do not settle there in the same numbers.
73 B.C.	The area around Herculaneum is threatened by the rebellion of **gladiators,** led by Spartacus. They defeat the Roman army but are eventually overcome and killed.
A.D.59	The riot in the amphitheater at Pompeii. In heavy fighting between Pompeians and people from Nuceria, several Nucerians are killed. The games are banned for ten years.
A.D.62	An earthquake badly damages both cities. Rebuilding begins immediately.
A.D.79	The eruption of Vesuvius destroys Pompeii and Herculaneum.
A.D.1594–1600	The site of Pompeii is discovered by the Italian architect Domenico Fontana, while cutting a channel to divert the course of a river. There is no serious attempt to explore the site.

A.D. 1709	The ruins of Herculaneum are discovered under the property of the Prince of Elboeuf, while a well is being dug. **Excavation** reveals marbles and sculptures.
A.D. 1738	The excavation of Herculaneum begins on the orders of Charles of Bourbon, King of Naples.
A.D. 1748	Charles orders the excavation of Pompeii.

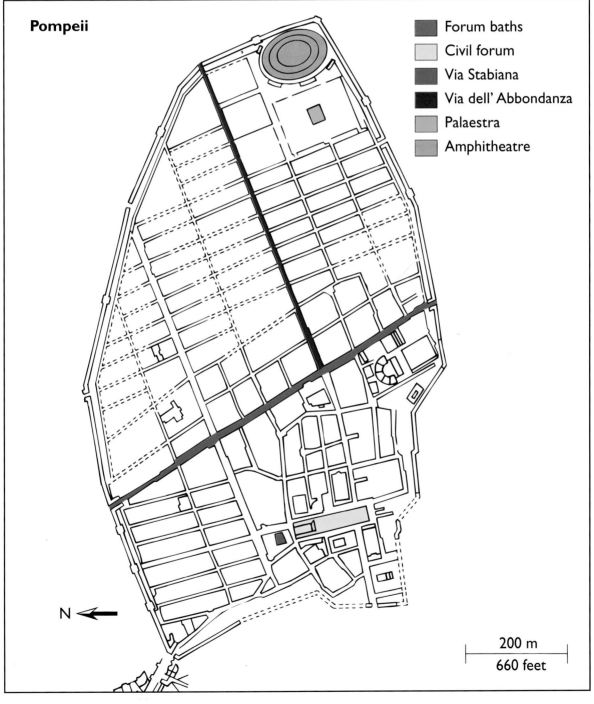

Pompeii

Legend:
- Forum baths
- Civil forum
- Via Stabiana
- Via dell' Abbondanza
- Palaestra
- Amphitheatre

N ←

200 m
660 feet

Glossary

aediles elected officials responsible for cleaning and repairing the streets, supervising water and sanitation, and organizing markets and the games in the amphitheater

amphitheater the great arena used for gladiatorial combats, animal fighting, and chariot racing

amphora pottery container that is narrow at the bottom and wide at the top but has a narrow neck

apodyterium dressing room at the public baths

archaeologist person who studies the past by looking at ancient ruins and remains

atrium large entrance hall of a house, usually partly covered and partly open to the sky

basilica building used for meetings of lawyers and the hearing of lawsuits; also the place where businessmen met and made deals.

caldarium hot room at the public baths

cockfighting fight between two birds as sport for the watchers

colonnade series of columns supporting a roof

duovirii elected magistrates of the town responsible for law and order

excavate to remove soil, especially over ancient ruins

forum large open space in a Roman town that was the social and business center of the town

frigidarium cold room at the public baths

fuller's earth fine clay mixed with water and used to clean cloth by trampling it underfoot

fullonica workshop for cleaning and dyeing cloth and clothes

garum strong-smelling sauce made from eggs and the fermented guts of fish

gladiator slave or prisoner of war who was trained to fight as public entertainment

graffiti slogans or other writing or drawings put on public walls

impluvium stone tank in the center of the atrium that collected rainwater coming through the opening in the roof

lararium small shrine where the household gods, called lares, were worshiped

macellum main market in the town where all types of fresh food were sold, including meat, fish, fruit, and vegetables

mosaic pattern or picture made from small pieces of colored glass, tiles, or stone

palaestrum gymnasium where young men went to get exercise, to train for athletic events, and to swim

pergola series of columns supporting a trellis over which plants can be grown

peristyle garden of a house, usually surrounded by columns and a veranda

potash a chemical used for bleaching

republic a country governed by an elected government rather than a king or queen

soda white powder, sodium carbonate, used in cleaning

sundial instrument that tells the time from the position of a shadow made by the sun

tepidarium warm room at the public baths

thermopolium inn where hot and cold wine and food were served, often providing entertainment and gambling games.

triclinium dining room of a house

trident spear with three prongs, like a fork

More Books to Read

Chapman, Gillian. *The Romans.* Des Plaines, Ill.: Heinemann Library, 1998.

Hicks, Peter. *Pompeii & Herculaneum.* Austin, Tex.: Raintree Steck-Vaughn Publishers, 1995.

Hodge, Susie. *Ancient Roman Art.* Des Plaines, Ill.: Heinemann Library, 1998.

Pompeii: The Day a City Was Buried. New York: DK Publishing, Incorporated, 1998.

Tanaka, Shelley. *The Buried City of Pompeii: I Was There.* New York: Hyperion Books for Children, 1997.

Index